CW01628937

What the
Teaches About Alcohol.

A Short Bible Study on the Biblical View of Wine

By

J.M.H van de Looverbosch

JvdL

Copyright © 2024 J.M.H. van de Looverbosch

Cover Design by J.M.H. van de Looverbosch

Publisher: JvdL

ISBN: 978-83-970755-0-4

All rights reserved. No part of this book may be reproduced without written permission of the copyright owner, except for the use of limited quotations for the purpose of book reviews.

All Scripture quotations, unless otherwise indicated, are taken from the New American Standard Bible - NASB 1995

NASB 1995

Scripture quotations taken from the (NASB®) New American Standard Bible®, Copyright © 1960, 1971, 1977, 1995 by The Lockman Foundation. Used by permission. All rights reserved. lockman.org

NKJV

Scripture taken from the New King James Version®. Copyright © 1982 by Thomas Nelson. Used by permission. All rights reserved.

ESV

Scripture quotations are from the ESV® Bible (The Holy Bible, English Standard Version®), copyright© 2001 by Crossway Bibles, a publishing ministry of Good News Publishers. Used by permission. All rights reserved.

Introduction

I've encountered many situations where people, and even pastors would say things like, "all positive references to wine in Scripture refer to non-alcoholic beverages". Over the years, I have participated in many Bible studies and read numerous journal articles, but none of them have addressed my current goal: an honest examination of what the Bible actually says regarding alcohol. This is a crucial lesson, and I believe many respected teachers frequently mishandle or depict it incorrectly.

Though I have great respect for godly teachers and biblical scholars, it appears that some teachers and even institutions stray from the holy text when discussing this specific subject. For instance, prior to enrolling in university to pursue a degree in theology, I attended a Bible college where I obtained a diploma in biblical studies. Upon completion, there was an opportunity to pursue ordination as a pastor. However, one of the requirements for ordination was abstaining from drinking alcohol. This condition deterred me from seeking ordination.

These experiences are the basis of this Bible study in which I want to show you the most important Bible verses about alcohol. Before we get started, let me make it clear that my goal is not to change your personal beliefs about alcohol. Please understand that I deeply respect and honor your decision to refrain from consuming alcohol due to your personal convictions.

The Biblical View of Wine:

The purpose of this study is straightforward: what does the Bible say about drinking? This dilemma arises because preachers often misinterpret the matter. Teachers may find it difficult to detect when their own customs are imposed on the text as a result of cultural influences from their community or background.

In this study, we will explore the Bible's positive verses that discuss alcohol in favorable terms, followed by an examination of its negative passages cautioning against its abuse. There seems to be a contradiction in the teachings, with some imposing unreasonable limits on Christians, while others discuss it informally, ignoring the grave cautions provided in Scripture.

Additionally, we will delve into discussions about the medical use of alcohol, referencing specific sections that present differing viewpoints on this topic. Finally, I hope to shed some light on the matter for those debating whether or not to drink alcohol.

Before we dive into our study, let's first turn to 2 Timothy 3:16–17: "*All Scripture is inspired by God and profitable for teaching, for reproof, for correction, for training in righteousness; so that the man of God may be adequate, equipped for every good work.*"

The Bible's authority to effect change and demand obedience stems from its divine origin — all Scripture is God-breathed. This divine authorship underscores God's authority over every aspect of life. To accept the Bible as God's authoritative Word is to acknowledge God's sovereignty over humanity.

The Holy Spirit inspired men to write the Bible and serves various purposes, including: teaching correct doctrine, rebuking and correcting deviations from truth, and guiding individuals back to obedience. Through stories, warnings, and instructions, both the Old and New Testaments address disobedience and offer guidance for righteous living.

The ultimate aim of the Bible's instruction, discipline, and training is not merely to occupy us, but to thoroughly equip us for every good work. By studying the Bible and relying on God's Spirit and the community of believers, we mature in faith and remain obedient to God's call. Neglecting the Scriptures jeopardizes our ability to serve God and others effectively, as they provide the guidance and empowerment needed for faithful service.

Overall, 2 Timothy 3:16-17 encapsulates the profound significance of Scripture as the source of divine inspiration and guidance and truth for believers, highlighting its relevance across diverse contexts and interpretations.

I referenced this Bible passage to underscore the significance of recognizing the Bible's authority in guiding teaching and correction. It serves as a reminder of the pivotal role Scripture plays in shaping our understanding of truth and guiding our paths. With this in mind, let's delve into the study.

The Positive References to Wine

In Deuteronomy 14, we encounter a passage that addresses the practice of presenting the firstfruits to the Lord. In the agrarian society of ancient Israel, after cultivating their fields, they would bring in the initial produce and celebrate a feast to honor the Lord, offering the firstfruits to God. Let's explore Deuteronomy 14:22–26:

"*You shall surely tithe all the produce from what you sow, which comes out of the field every year. "You shall eat in the presence of the Lord your God, at the place where He chooses to establish His name, the tithe of your grain, your new wine, your oil, and the firstborn of your herd and your flock, so that you may learn to fear the Lord your God always. "If the distance is so great for you that you are not able to bring the tithe, since the place where the Lord your God chooses to set His name is too far away from you when the Lord your God blesses you, then you shall exchange it for money, and bind the money in your hand and go to the place which the Lord your God chooses. "You may spend the money for whatever your heart desires: for oxen, or sheep, or wine, or strong drink, or whatever your heart desires; and there you shall eat in the presence of the Lord your God and rejoice, you and your household."*

Some have attempted to interpret this passage by suggesting that the term "*wine*" may not refer to an alcoholic beverage, but the Hebrew language used in verse 26 is quite explicit. It mentions " *wine, or strong drink*" leaving little room for ambiguity. This undeniably includes alcoholic content. Some argue that it could be non-alcoholic due to the timing of the first fruits and the pressing of grapes. However, given that this celebration occurs once a year, in April or May, while in Israel, the grape harvest unfolded in late August or September. The likelihood of fermentation is evident. Thus, the reference to "*wine, or strong drink*" in this context unquestionably implies an alcoholic beverage.

The essential point to grasp here is that if you've been exposed to teachings suggesting that the wine mentioned in this passage is not alcoholic, such assertions are not accurate. Our theological foundations must be rooted in the truth presented in Scripture, rather than shaped based on what might be perceived as safer for people's lives. Therefore, we need to engage with the actual teachings of the Bible.

In Deuteronomy 14, the passage illustrates the act of spending money on wine, or strong drink of one's choosing to enjoy it in the context of a feast unto the Lord. While this is not explicitly centered on alcohol or wine, it includes them, and although intoxication is discouraged, the enjoyment of such beverages as part of their celebration is sanctioned. It is important to note that the option to drink wine is not obligatory, but it is a permissible choice.

Moving on to another positive passage, Numbers 15:7, "*and for the drink offering you shall offer one-third of a hin of wine as a soothing aroma to the LORD*", this verse instructs the offering of one-third of a hin of wine as a drink offering, creating a sweet aroma for the Lord.

In the Hebrew language, various words are used for alcoholic drinks or wine. One of these terms refers to new or sweet wine, which may refer to a lower percentage of alcohol. Another term, yayin, denotes a more aged wine and unequivocally signifies a fermented beverage.

Numbers 15:7 unequivocally endorses the offering of fermented drink as a sweet aroma to the Lord, dispelling any notion that it might refer to grape juice. This passage signifies permission in the Old Testament law to present alcohol in this manner, recognizing that we now embrace the fullness of the New Covenant rather than the shadows of past rituals. While we may not adhere to these specific practices, the principles behind them remain instructive.

It's crucial to grasp the principle embedded in this passage: God allowed the offering of wine as a sweet aroma. For those who may have grown up with the notion that alcohol is inherently sinful, a careful examination of the Scriptures redirects us from a legalistic perspective. The scriptural message is clear: God asks for the offering of the best, emphasizing that it should be without spot or blemish. This is not an endorsement of offering displeasing or detestable things to God. Instead, it encourages presenting the finest as a sweet aroma to the Lord.

Acknowledging that negative passages about alcohol will follow, it's important to assure those who harbor reservations about alcohol that a balanced view will be presented. The goal is to faithfully convey what the Bible communicates, even if it challenges personal inclinations. I am committed to presenting a fair and accurate perspective on the topic.

Genesis 14:18, "*And Melchizedek king of Salem brought out bread and wine; now he was a priest of God Most High*." In this verse we encounter the term "yayin," indicating a definitively fermented beverage with alcohol content, though not as potent as stronger spirits like scotch or vodka. It refers to a truly fermented drink, akin to wine. The verse narrates how Melchizedek, the king of Salem and the priest of God Most High, presents bread and wine to Abraham. This symbolic act is widely understood as a portrayal of Jesus in the Old Testament, prefiguring the Communion and the sacrificial body and blood of Christ for our sins. Notably, the inclusion of wine in this sacred moment does not detract from its significance, and it does not lead to drunkenness.

Moving on to another positive passage, Psalm 104:15, "*And wine which makes man's heart glad, So that he may make his face glisten with oil, And food which sustains man's heart*." This Psalm enumerates the blessings God has bestowed upon humankind. While addressing various gifts, the verse highlights wine as something that gladdens the heart of man. Once again, the term used is "yayin," affirming that the reference is to an alcoholic or intoxicating beverage. Psalm 104, in its acknowledgment of wine as a blessing, challenges any negative associations one might have with alcohol.

For those finding these passages challenging, I am committed to presenting what the Bible communicates, even if it challenges personal beliefs. Psalm 104 makes it explicit that wine, in the context of God's blessings, is intended to bring joy to the heart of man.

This revelation might be enlightening as it becomes evident that wine is intended to be a blessing, and the text emphasizes not only the substance itself but also its effects on the human heart. Notably, Psalm 104:15 goes beyond acknowledging wine as a blessing; it explicitly states that wine "*makes man's heart glad*" This inclusion of both the beverage and its effects challenges the notion that enjoying the effects of wine is inherently sinful. The text seems to imply that the blessing of wine encompasses both its consumption and the positive impact it has on one's mood.

The hermeneutic approach employed here underscores the interconnectedness of the substance and its effects, aligning with the broader concept presented in Psalm 104. The verse links oil to make one's face shine, bread to strengthen the heart, and wine to bring joy to the heart. This view suggests that wine, in moderate amounts, aligns with a biblical perspective of blessing. It's crucial to understand that God approves of alcohol's initial effects, such as elevating mood. However, the subsequent, more profound effects are cautioned against, marking the boundary where further alcohol consumption may lead into sinful territory. In essence, moderate drinking, within biblical guidelines, is portrayed as a blessing from God.

This may come as surprising, but it's essential to acknowledge what the text conveys. Let's focus on understanding what the Bible truly communicates about alcohol and allow God to shape our perspectives. While you have the right to place additional restrictions on yourself, let's avoid imposing our own personal convictions on others if they are unsupported by the Bible.

Moving forward, we might find that there are two distinct groups, one appreciating the first half of the study and another favoring the latter. Currently, we're still in the first half. Proverbs 3:7-10, "*Do not be wise in your own eyes; Fear the LORD and turn away from evil. It will be healing to your body And refreshment to your bones. Honor the LORD from your wealth And from the first of all your produce; So your barns will be filled with plenty And your vats will overflow with new wine.*" Proverbs 3:7-10 advises against self-reliance, urging one to fear the Lord and shun evil. Following God's guidance in these areas is depicted as a blessing, promoting health and strength.

Notably, honoring the Lord with possessions, including the first fruits, is linked to abundance, with barns filled and vats overflowing with new wine. Once more, wine is portrayed as a divine blessing bestowed by God. Throughout biblical texts wine emerges as a symbol of God's generosity and provision.

Proverbs 9:1-6, "*Wisdom has built her house, She has hewn out her seven pillars; She has prepared her food, she has mixed her wine; She has also set her table; She has sent out her maidens, she calls From the tops of the heights of the city: "Whoever is naive, let him turn in here!" To him who lacks understanding she says, "Come, eat of my food And drink of the wine I have mixed. "Forsake your folly and live, And proceed in the way of understanding.*" Proverbs 9:1-6 employs symbolic language to illustrate wisdom, using the metaphor of a feast with mixed wine. Symbolic or not, wine cannot symbolize blessing if it's inherently evil. This metaphorical usage points towards abundance, benefits, and having more than enough.

Isaiah 25:6, "*The LORD of hosts will prepare a lavish banquet for all peoples on this mountain; A banquet of aged wine, choice pieces with marrow, And refined, aged wine.*" The passage describes a future time, likely referring to the millennial reign. The verse speaks of a feast prepared by the Lord of hosts on a mountain, featuring choice pieces and well-refined wines. The mention of "well-refined wines" indicates aged wines with a discernible alcohol content. This imagery portrays a positive and abundant scene, suggesting that the use of wine in this context is intended as a blessing.

Throughout my years of studying this concept, I have grappled with the idea that wine and alcohol are intended by God to be blessings for humanity. Despite witnessing instances of abuse, I have come to recognize that the Bible presents wine as a gift from God to be enjoyed responsibly. The symbolic representation of wine as a component of a divine feast reinforces its association with blessing and joy.

In essence, while acknowledging the potential for misuse, the Bible consistently portrays wine as a symbol of God's provision and goodness. It is a reminder that when used appropriately, wine can enhance fellowship, celebration, and gratitude in accordance with God's intentions. The Bible, in its wisdom, remains unchanged and trustworthy.

Isaiah 1:21-22 (ESV), "*How the faithful city has become a whore, she who was full of justice! Righteousness lodged in her, but now murderers. Your silver has become dross, your best wine mixed with water.*" Isaiah paints a somber picture of a once faithful city that has deviated, likening it to a harlot. The city, once a haven of justice and righteousness, now harbors murderers. The metaphor continues with the degradation of silver to dross and the dilution of wine with water. This dilution, far from a celebratory mixing, is portrayed as a lamentable state—watering down the wine is considered a negative development.

In the New Testament, we turn to John 2, where Jesus performs his first miracle at the wedding in Cana. Some argue that this miraculous transformation of water into wine was non-alcoholic, citing ancient writers who claimed that the best wine had lost its alcohol content through filtration. However, historical research suggests that the Romans, contemporaries of that time, commonly watered down their strong wine, creating a consistency akin to modern-day beer.

Conversely, it is posited that the Jews, who had a distinct culture, may not have adopted this practice, considering it uncouth to dilute their wine. Given the Jewish context of the wedding at Cana, relying solely on Roman practices might not accurately reflect the Jewish approach to wine consumption during that period.

Let's examine the remarks of the master of the feast in John 2:9-10, "*When the headwaiter tasted the water which had become wine, and did not know where it came from (but the servants who had drawn the water knew), the headwaiter called the bridegroom, and said to him, "Every man serves the good wine first, and when the people have drunk freely, then he serves the poorer wine; but you have kept the good wine until now.*" After tasting the water miraculously turned into wine by Jesus, the master of the feast, unaware of its origin, summoned the bridegroom. He conveyed, "*Every man serves the good wine first, and when the people have drunk freely, then he serves the poorer wine; but you have kept the good wine until now.*".

Engaging in a purely hermeneutical study, this exploration aims at understanding the scriptural context rather than personal preferences. The text's clarity suggests that the wine Jesus produced was unquestionably alcoholic. How do we discern this? The master of the feast typically serves the best wine first, reserving the lesser quality for later when the guests have become somewhat intoxicated. The Greek phrase used implies a degree of intoxication. In comparing the wine Jesus made to the customary good wine, the master of the feast acknowledges its excellence. This implies that Jesus's wine was of high quality, capable of causing intoxication. The evidence is intrinsic to the text, rendering additional studies in ancient Greek or Roman cultures unnecessary. The straightforward reading of the passage suffices.

It's crucial to clarify that using this text to excuse or downplay the sinfulness of drunkenness is misguided. While Jesus made alcoholic wine for the event, it doesn't imply approval of or indifference toward drunkenness. The Bible, in various instances, addresses the serious consequences and admonitions associated with drunkenness, which we will explore shortly.

In Matthew 11:19, Jesus responds to accusations, with some calling him a bad influence. The passage states, "*The Son of Man came eating and drinking, and they say, 'Behold, a gluttonous man and a drunkard, a friend of tax collectors and sinners!' Yet wisdom is vindicated by her deeds.*" Now, if Jesus only consumed grape juice, such accusations of being a drunkard wouldn't hold. Therefore, it can be inferred that Jesus did partake in drinking, ensuring that he never crossed the boundaries of appropriateness or became even slightly intoxicated. The emphasis here is on moderation, suggesting that Jesus consumed wine responsibly. These examples make a strong case for the idea that God intended wine, when consumed in moderation, to be a blessing for humanity.

The Negative References to Wine.

Now, let's delve into the negative passages. One such passage is found in Proverbs 20:1, stating, " *Wine is a mocker, strong drink a brawler, And whoever is intoxicated by it is not wise.*" This verse underscores the transformative nature of alcohol consumption, turning individuals into mockers and brawlers. Under its influence, inhibitions are lost, leading to foolish speech, criticism, and a heightened likelihood of engaging in physical or emotional conflicts. The verse concludes by emphasizing that being intoxicated by alcohol is an unwise choice, highlighting the inherent danger. While alcohol may be intended as a blessing, its potential to lead individuals astray is a serious concern. If you found the positive aspects of the study resonant, it's crucial to recognize the significance of these cautionary passages.

Moving forward, Proverbs 21:17 provides another cautionary perspective: "*He who loves pleasure will become a poor man; He who loves wine and oil will not become rich.*" This verse links an excessive pursuit of pleasure, particularly in the form of wine and oil, to poverty. It serves as a reminder that an excessive attachment to indulgences can have detrimental consequences on one's well-being and financial stability. These verses collectively underscore the importance of temperance and wise choices when it comes to the consumption of alcohol. Proverbs 23:29-35 provides a stark depiction of the consequences of excessive drinking, verse 29: *"Who has woe? Who has sorrow? Who has contentions? Who has complaining? Who has wounds without cause? Who has redness of eyes? Those who linger long over wine, Those who go to taste mixed wine.*" The vivid portrayal in 33-31 continues with a caution against fixating on wine, "*Those who linger long over wine, Those who go to taste mixed wine. Do not look on the wine when it is red, When it sparkles in the cup, When it goes down smoothly;*" The message is clear: if you find yourself craving wine excessively, it signals a potential problem.

The symptoms listed—woe, sorrow, contentions, complaining, wounds without cause, and redness of eyes—serve as warning signs. If your consumption of alcohol leads to these issues in your life, it indicates an imbalance. The emphasis here is not a blanket condemnation of all alcohol consumption; rather, it targets those who excessively indulge, lingering too long at the wine. The advice is specific: if you observe these negative outcomes in your life, perhaps the best course of action is to abstain entirely. The scripture suggests that for those who struggle with the abuse of alcohol, refraining from looking at it altogether may be the wisest choice.

Verses 32-33 reinforces the point: "*At the last it bites like a serpent And stings like a viper. Your eyes will see strange things And your mind will utter perverse things.*" This vivid imagery serves as a metaphor for the eventual harmful effects of prolonged and excessive alcohol consumption, likening it to the bite of a serpent. It emphasizes the destructive nature of overindulgence, urging caution and moderation in one's relationship with alcohol. It's intriguing how even secular observations about alcohol align with certain biblical truths. Excessive alcohol consumption often leads people to express negative behaviors and utter inappropriate, selfish, and ungodly words. This manifestation is reflective of the sinful nature of humanity, which becomes more susceptible to control when under the influence of alcohol.

The warning in the scripture about the heart uttering perverse things emphasizes the undesirable outcomes of consuming too much alcohol. Verse 34-35, "*And you will be like one who lies down in the middle of the sea, Or like one who lies down on the top of a mast. "They struck me, but I did not become ill; They beat me, but I did not know it. When shall I awake? I will seek another drink.*" The metaphorical description of someone lying down in the middle of the sea or on top of a boat's mast exemplifies the confusion that an intoxicated person experiences. This individual, despite being struck and beaten, remains oblivious to the pain, highlighting the impaired judgment that accompanies excessive drinking. The Bible further addresses the issue of waking up with a craving for another drink, signaling a problematic relationship with alcohol. If one finds oneself numb to pain, speaking sinful words, or struggling with balance and coordination after drinking, it serves as a biblical indicator that they have consumed too much.

The idea that individuals are able to precisely measure their level of intoxication is called into question by the paragraph, which also highlights the necessity of establishing more stringent limits and restrictions. In the end, the scriptural cues offer insights into what are considered to be excessive amounts of alcohol intake and advocate a careful and responsible attitude to drinking that is based on biblical principles.

Proverbs 31:4-7, "*It is not for kings, O Lemuel, It is not for kings to drink wine, Or for rulers to desire strong drink, For they will drink and forget what is decreed, And pervert the rights of all the afflicted. Give strong drink to him who is perishing, And wine to him whose life is bitter.*

Let him drink and forget his poverty And remember his trouble no more.", in these verses, a mother imparts wisdom to her son, Lemuel, advising against the consumption of wine and intoxicating drinks, especially for kings and princes. The counsel is rooted in the potential consequences of impaired judgment and the perversion of justice.

The passage doesn't necessarily imply that kings or princes should never drink wine, but it underscores the inappropriateness of doing so in specific contexts, particularly when carrying out their responsibilities. The concern is that partaking in alcohol may lead to forgetfulness of the law and compromise their ability to administer justice fairly, especially for the afflicted.

This principle extends to situations where individuals hold positions of significant responsibility, such as political leaders or pastors. Engaging in alcohol consumption before making critical decisions or handling matters of importance could potentially impair judgment and compromise the integrity of those responsibilities.

The overarching idea is to exercise discernment in situations where sound judgment is crucial, emphasizing that certain duties and roles may necessitate abstinence from alcohol to ensure clarity, wisdom, and the fair execution of justice.

In Leviticus 10:9, the context involves the sons of Aaron, Nadab and Abihu, who, after drinking, entered the tabernacle to minister to God with improper incense, resulting in their death. God then commands Aaron, "*Do not drink wine or strong drink, neither you nor your sons with you, when you come into the tent of meeting, so that you will not die—it is a perpetual statute throughout your generations—*" This underscores the prohibition of alcohol during sacred moments and emphasizes the gravity of entering the presence of God while under the influence.

Ezekiel 44:21 reiterates this principle, stating: "*Nor shall any of the priests drink wine when they enter the inner court.*", highlighting the sanctity of certain worship contexts.

Moving to the New Testament, Ephesians 5:17-18, "*So then do not be foolish, but understand what the will of the Lord is. And do not get drunk with wine, for that is dissipation, but be filled with the Spirit.*" These verses advise believers not to be unwise but to understand the will of the Lord. It explicitly warns against being drunk with wine, which leads to dissipation, instead encouraging believers to be filled with the Spirit. This passage reinforces the principle that Christians should avoid drunkenness altogether, promoting a sober and spiritually aware lifestyle.

In summary, these verses emphasize the importance of discernment in specific situations, such as entering the presence of God or engaging in worship. Moreover, the New Testament emphasizes the general prohibition of drunkenness for believers, promoting a lifestyle characterized by spiritual awareness rather than indulgence in intoxicating substances.

If individuals believe that occasional getting drunk is acceptable as long as it doesn't become habitual, the scriptural perspective is clear, it is considered a serious sin. The Bible unequivocally states that being drunk, whether occasionally or habitually, is incompatible with a Christian lifestyle.

In essence, the scriptural guidance is straightforward: Christians should always seek to be filled with the Holy Spirit, just as they should consistently avoid drunkenness. These two states are incompatible with one another, suggesting that being drunk makes it impossible to be under the influence of the Holy Spirit. Therefore, the call to avoid drunkenness is constant and extends to all aspects of a believer's life.

In practical terms, drinking too much not only violates biblical principles but also damages one's relationship with Jesus in an immediate and tangible way. The Scriptures emphasize that being drunk hinders the ability to be filled with the Holy Spirit, reinforcing the seriousness of this sin in the context of one's spiritual walk.

For those who choose to exercise the liberty to drink within biblical guidelines, there is a heightened responsibility to be vigilant against crossing the line into drunkenness. Unlike those who abstain from alcohol, individuals who partake must be especially rigorous in discerning the boundary between moderation and excess. This heightened concern is driven by the recognition that the act of drinking, if not approached with caution, can lead to a serious breach in the relationship between the individual and God.

In conclusion, the scriptural stance is clear: Christians, particularly those who choose to drink, must be conscientious and vigilant about avoiding drunkenness, as it directly impacts their walk with God. The call is not only to enjoy liberty but also to exercise it responsibly, with a profound awareness of the potential spiritual consequences of excessive drinking.

The New King James Version translates Hosea 4:11 as follows: "*Harlotry, wine, and new wine enslave the heart.*" delivering a powerful message about the enslaving nature of wine and new wine, highlighting the potential for addiction. The biblical standpoint emphasizes the negative consequences of becoming enslaved to such substances, marking it as an undesirable outcome. In correlation, 1 Corinthians 6:12 (ESV), *"All things are lawful for me," but not all things are helpful. "All things are lawful for me," but I will not be dominated by anything.*" This text provides a guiding principle applicable to this context: while all things may be permissible, not all things are beneficial, and one should refrain from being brought under the power of anything.

This principle serves as a stark reminder that if wine or any substance begins to exert control over an individual, leading to enslavement, it becomes a serious problem. The verse urges self-awareness and personal responsibility, especially for those struggling with drinking problems. In such cases, individuals are encouraged to confront the issue head-on, without waiting for external interventions. It's a call to maturity, urging self-reflection and the acknowledgment of the problem for the sake of personal growth and well-being.

The broader societal implications of alcoholism, including statistics on drinking-related issues such as accidents, are acknowledged, but the scriptural emphasis is on the personal responsibility to avoid being brought under the power of anything. Hosea and 1 Corinthians together present a strong biblical warning against the enslaving nature of substances like wine, emphasizing the need for self-awareness, responsibility, and avoidance of harmful dependencies.

Habakkuk 2:15-16, *"Woe to you who make your neighbors drink, Who mix in your venom even to make them drunk So as to look on their nakedness! "You will be filled with disgrace rather than honor. Now you yourself drink and expose your own nakedness. The cup in the Lord's right hand will come around to you, And utter disgrace will come upon your glory.*" This passage serves as a stern warning against the misuse of alcohol to exploit and manipulate others. The verse declares a "*woe*" upon those who give drink to their neighbors, pressuring them to consume it excessively with the sinister intent of witnessing their subsequent shame or nakedness. This misuse of alcohol is condemned as an act of manipulation and a means to exploit the vulnerability of others.

The verse points to the moral culpability of those who seek to take advantage of individuals by encouraging excessive drinking, leading to behaviors that one might exploit for personal gain or amusement. It highlights the unethical nature of using alcohol as a tool to strip others of their inhibitions, creating a situation where individuals might act in ways they would not otherwise. The Bible warns that those who engage in this kind of behavior will bring shame upon themselves as a result of their actions.

In Gen 19:32, "*Come, let us make our father drink wine, and let us lie with him that we may preserve our family through our father.*", Lot's daughters used a similar tactic, providing their father with alcohol to engage in inappropriate actions, serves as an illustrative example of the serious consequences of such manipulation. The verse from Habakkuk stands as a divine condemnation of those who exploit others through the misuse of alcohol, emphasizing the importance of ethical and responsible behavior in interpersonal relationships.

Another illustration is that of David, who manipulated Uriah through alcohol to conceal his own wrongdoing. This sobering example highlights the misuse of alcohol to achieve unethical ends. God's disapproval, as evident in passages like Habakkuk 2:15, signifies the severe consequences of such actions.

Isaiah 28:7 (NKJV), "*But they also have erred through wine, And through intoxicating drink are out of the way; The priest and the prophet have erred through intoxicating drink, They are swallowed up by wine, They are out of the way through intoxicating drink; They err in vision, they stumble in judgment.*" This verse underscores the negative impact of intoxicating drinks on individuals, including priests and prophets. It describes how these religious leaders have erred in vision and stumbled in judgment due to the influence of alcohol. The verse emphasizes that the consumption of intoxicating drinks has led them astray from the right path, causing their lives to deviate from obedience to God.

In this context, the text portrays a warning against the harmful effects of alcohol, especially when it leads individuals, including those in positions of spiritual leadership, away from righteousness and sound judgment. It highlights the potential dangers of allowing alcohol to impair one's vision and judgment, leading to serious consequences for both personal conduct and spiritual leadership.

Isaiah 5:11, "*Woe to those who rise early in the morning that they may pursue strong drink, Who stay up late in the evening that wine may inflame them!*" This verse provides a strong warning against those who habitually pursue intoxicating drinks from morning until night. The passage highlights the detrimental effects of excessive and continuous drinking, portraying it as a behavior that is worthy of condemnation. Rising early in the morning to indulge in intoxicating drinks and persisting in this activity throughout the day, is depicted as a shameful and foolish practice.

The emphasis on the persistence and dedication to drinking suggests a pattern of behavior that is not aligned with God's wisdom and guidance. The use of the term "*woe*" signals a divine disapproval of such conduct.

In the context of this verse, it becomes clear that God views the continuous pursuit of intoxicating drinks as detrimental to individuals and contrary to the principles of righteous living. It serves as a warning against the foolishness of putting excessive drinking ahead of a life lived in wisdom and in accordance with godly values.

Isaiah 5:22, "*Woe to those who are heroes in drinking wine And valiant men in mixing strong drink*" This verse issues a powerful and severe warning, proclaiming "*woe*" to those who are heroes at drinking wine and valiant for mixing intoxicating drink. The verse condemns individuals who take pride in their ability to consume large quantities of alcohol and those who excel in the preparation of strong and intoxicating drinks. The use of the term "*woe*" emphasizes a divine judgment and disapproval of such behavior.

The world often glorifies and boasts about one's capacity to handle alcohol, engaging in drinking contests and similar activities. However, from a Christian perspective, the verse strongly condemns such practices as wickedness and evil in the eyes of God. It challenges the cultural norms that celebrate excessive drinking and urges believers to approach alcohol with caution and a heightened sense of responsibility.

For those who choose to exercise the liberty to drink, the warning in Isaiah 5:22 underscores the need for vigilance and a serious attitude toward the potential pitfalls associated with alcohol. The emphasis is on avoiding pride in one's capacity for alcohol consumption and recognizing the inherent dangers of excessive drinking.

Galatians 5:21, "*envying, drunkenness, carousing, and things like these, of which I forewarn you, just as I have forewarned you, that those who practice such things will not inherit the kingdom of God.*" This verse provides a list of behaviors that are considered works of the flesh, and it explicitly mentions drunkenness as one of them. The verse warns that those who practice such things will not inherit the kingdom of God. This implies that habitual engagement in these sinful behaviors, including drunkenness, is incompatible with the characteristics of those who belong to the kingdom of God.

It's important to note that the emphasis is on the consistent practice or lifestyle of these behaviors. The passage does not suggest that an isolated incident of drunkenness automatically excludes someone from inheriting the kingdom of God. Instead, it highlights a pattern of behavior that goes against the values and principles of God's kingdom.

For believers, this serves as a strong admonition to turn away from practices that are contrary to the teachings of Christ. It underscores the transformative power of faith in Christ, urging believers to live in accordance with the Spirit rather than the flesh. Ultimately, the passage encourages a life characterized by the fruits of the Spirit, as outlined in the preceding verses of Galatians 5.

1 Corinthians 6:10, "*nor thieves, nor the covetous, nor drunkards, nor revilers, nor*

swindlers, will inherit the kingdom of God." This passage also provides a strong warning against various sinful behaviors, including drunkenness, stating that those who engage in such practices will not inherit the kingdom of God. This underscores the gravity of the issue and emphasizes the need for believers to live in accordance with God's standards.

The passage aligns with the broader biblical teaching that emphasizes the importance of holy living and the pursuit of righteousness. While acknowledging the potential blessings and appropriate uses of alcohol, it highlights the serious consequences of misusing it, particularly through excessive drinking and drunkenness.

For believers, these warnings serve as a call to align their lives with the transformative power of the gospel and to avoid practices that are contrary to God's will. The passages underscore the significance of living in obedience to God's commands and the ethical standards set forth in the Scriptures.

Psalm 75:8, "*For a cup is in the hand of the Lord, and the wine foams; It is well mixed, and He pours out of this; Surely all the wicked of the earth must drain and drink down its dregs.*" This Psalm verse presents a symbolic use of wine to convey the concept of divine judgment. The image of the Lord pouring out a cup of fully mixed red wine represents the pouring out of judgment on the wicked. This metaphorical use of wine is consistent with other biblical passages that employ similar symbolism to represent God's righteous judgment.

The Christian Lifestyle.

It's essential to consider both the positive and negative aspects of the biblical teachings on wine and alcohol. While there are verses highlighting the potential blessings and positive uses of wine, there are also warnings against misuse, excessive drinking, and the negative consequences associated with it. The diverse biblical perspectives aim to provide a comprehensive understanding of the topic and guide believers in making wise and righteous choices.

Balancing these perspectives enables individuals to appreciate the richness of biblical teachings on the subject of wine, recognizing both its potential for blessing and the dangers of its misuse. Ultimately, the Scriptures call for discernment, moderation, and adherence to God's principles in all aspects of life.

Luke 1:15, "*For he will be great in the sight of the Lord; and he will drink no wine or liquor, and he will be filled with the Holy Spirit while yet in his mother's womb.*" The verse highlights a unique aspect of John the Baptist's life, where he was set apart to be great in the sight of the Lord and was to abstain from both wine and strong drink. This particular calling for John was a part of his consecration and devotion to God, emphasizing a lifestyle of separation and being filled with the Holy Spirit.

It's crucial to recognize the diversity of God's callings and instructions for individuals. While John the Baptist was set apart to abstain from wine, Jesus, on the other hand, partook in it without sin. This illustrates that God may call different people to different standards based on their specific roles and purposes in His plan.

This diversity should lead to a balanced perspective within the Christian community. Some may feel led to abstain from certain practices, such as drinking wine, as a personal conviction or as a specific calling from God. At the same time, others may responsibly partake in such activities to the glory of God. The key is not to impose personal convictions as universal rules but to respect the diversity of God's guidance for individual lives. In Titus 2 (NKJV), guidance is provided for both older men and older women, considering the cultural context of maturity. The passage emphasizes the importance of aligning one's conduct with sound doctrine. It states, "*But as for you, speak the things which are proper for sound doctrine: that the older men be sober, reverent, temperate, sound in faith, in love, in patience.*"

Similarly, the older women are encouraged to exhibit reverence in their behavior, avoiding slander and refraining from excessive wine consumption. The passage suggests they should serve as teachers of good things. Notably, it doesn't advocate complete abstinence from wine, as it doesn't say "no wine at all," but rather advises against giving in to excessive wine consumption.

These instructions reflect specific guidance for leaders, including bishops, elders, and deacons, underscoring the importance of their exemplary behavior in maintaining a community rooted in sound doctrine.

In 1 Timothy chapter 3, specific character qualities are outlined for those in leadership positions within the church. The bishop or elder is instructed not to be given over to wine, to be non-violent, not greedy for money, gentle, not quarrelsome, and not covetous. These qualities underscore the importance of godly character in church leadership. If an individual regularly compromises in the area of wine consumption, they are deemed disqualified for such a position. This disqualification is not a matter of others having the liberty to compromise, but rather a recognition that leaders in the church must exhibit a higher standard of character.

In 1 Timothy 3:8 (NKJV), requirements are set for deacons. "*Likewise deacons must be reverent, not double-tongued, not given to much wine, not greedy for money,*" These guidelines emphasize the importance of avoiding certain qualities and behaviors that may compromise their effectiveness in serving as deacons. The example of a pastor getting drunk, which would result in disqualification, highlights the seriousness of such issues. This underscores that the abuse of alcohol is a grave matter in the eyes of God, requiring the sacrifice of Jesus, and should be acknowledged with due seriousness.

Wine as a Medicine.

Luke 10:33-34, "*But a Samaritan, who was on a journey, came upon him; and when he saw him, he felt compassion, and came to him and bandaged up his wounds, pouring oil and wine on them; and he put him on his own beast, and brought him to an inn and took care of him.*" The Good Samaritan applied oil and wine to the injuries of the victim assaulted by robbers. Wine served as a remedy, contributing to the healing of wounds.

1 Timothy 5:23, "*No longer drink water exclusively, but use a little wine for the sake of your stomach and your frequent ailments.*" Here Paul provides advice to Timothy, acknowledging his usual abstention from wine. However, due to Timothy's stomach issues and frequent infirmities during his travels, Paul recommends a departure from his typical abstinence. Paul suggests incorporating a small amount of wine into water, possibly as a form of purification to address potential water-related bacterial concerns.[1] This adjustment in Timothy's

behavior is not a departure from his usual practice but a targeted and temporary measure to alleviate health challenges while on his travels. The passage underscores the practical considerations and flexibility needed in addressing specific circumstances, even for individuals who typically abstain from alcohol.

In Proverbs 31, after the initial warning about kings and princes abstaining from wine to maintain clear judgment, the passage takes an intriguing turn in verses 6 and 7. It suggests giving strong drink to those who are perishing or wine to those whose life is bitter. The text appears to be addressing individuals in dire circumstances or facing imminent death.

The specific wording says, "*Give strong drink to him who is perishing, And wine to him whose life is bitter. Let him drink and forget his poverty And remember his trouble no more.*"

Rather than an endorsement of using alcohol to cope with poverty or bitterness in a casual manner, the passage seems to acknowledge the harsh realities of life, where individuals facing imminent death or enduring intense emotional pain might find momentary solace in the numbing effects of strong drink or wine. It's a nuanced and specific scenario, emphasizing the complexities of human suffering and the

---

[1] Robert Stein, "Wine-Drinking in New Testament Times," *Christianity Today*, 20 June 1975, 10.

potential temporary relief that alcohol might provide in such extreme circumstances. I'm curious, have you ever found yourself by someone's deathbed? Would you consider withholding any medication that could ease their pain? Personally, I wouldn't.

Towards the end, the focus shifts to making the person as comfortable as possible. At that juncture, family members often express, "You don't need to be sober-minded right now; we just want to help you through this." Interestingly, there seems to be a biblical precedent for this compassionate approach found in Proverbs: "*Give strong drink to him who is perishing.*" This suggests that there might be situations where it's acceptable, even advisable, for someone facing the end of life to experience the soothing effects of substances, whether it's alcohol or medicinal aids like morphine. In these tremendously challenging moments, where there's no turning back, the aim is to alleviate their suffering. It appears that God understands and allows for a medicinal use, recognizing the exceptional circumstances of someone on the brink of death. This biblical perspective offers a well-rounded teaching, providing room for compassionate care, particularly in hospice or end-of-life situations. Of course, this compassionate approach needs careful consideration to avoid potential misuse, ensuring that it serves the genuine purpose of easing the person's distress rather than being exploited for personal reasons. The key is to strike a balance, recognizing the potential for abuse while still acknowledging the value of providing comfort in specific, challenging circumstances.

Conclusion.

Let's bring this Bible study to a conclusion. Returning to Romans 14, a chapter that has delved into various matters, including the topic of alcohol, specifically in verse 21, it emphasizes a crucial principle: "*It is good not to eat meat or to drink wine, or to do anything by which your brother stumbles.*" This statement suggests that, at least temporarily and especially in the presence of a brother or sister who might be adversely affected, it's wise to abstain from such activities. This approach aligns with the idea of avoiding actions that could potentially harm or offend others, demonstrating sensitivity to their convictions. It underscores the importance of considering the impact of our choices on those around us and exercising prudence in our conduct.

Let’s turn to 1 Corinthians 10, one of our final passages for this study. Specifically, 1 Corinthians 10:30-32 provides a well-balanced perspective on the issue at hand. This passage addresses both those who partake in drinking and thank the Lord for it and those who abstain, highlighting the importance of mutual respect, appreciation, and avoiding attempts to change one another.

Verse 30, states: "*If I partake with thankfulness, why am I slandered concerning that for which I give thanks?*" The emphasis here is on approaching eating and drinking with gratitude, doing everything to the glory of God. Whether one enjoys a drink in acknowledgment of God's blessing or refrains from it as an expression of freedom from bondage, both actions can be done to honor and glorify God.

However, verse 32 introduces an additional layer to the discussion by stating, "*Give no offense either to the Jews or to the Greeks or to the church of God.*" This verse emphasizes the cultural context, recognizing that different cultures may have varying perspectives on drinking. Paul, having engaged with both Jewish and Greek cultures, emphasizes the importance of not causing offense in these cultural contexts.

In essence, the teaching transcends specific cultural norms and aims to be applicable to Christians in various cultural settings. As believers, the challenge lies in applying these principles within our own cultural contexts, respecting the beliefs and values of those around us while honoring God in our choices.

I like to emphasize that if your heart is dedicated to serving Jesus with a balanced perspective on the matter, you are likely on the right track. For those inclined towards liberty, a gentle reminder to temper it, and for those leaning towards abstinence, a suggestion to ease up in their attitude towards others. While I didn't delve into details about ancient wine and its alcohol content, I stressed that the focus is not on the strength of the drink but rather on how it impacts an individual. The crux of the matter is maintaining sobriety while being able to appreciate the effects of alcohol within God's liberating framework for His glory. This Bible study aims to shed light on a perspective not commonly taught, and I hope it serves as a blessing. It is my belief that, in some instances, pastors may inadvertently restrict the liberties of the body of Christ due to a lack of trust, and I advocate for a more balanced approach, letting God's Word guide us without becoming unnecessary filters for the congregation's freedoms.

Facts:

The primary terms for wine are the Hebrew "yayin," the Aramaic "*ḥ*ᵃ*mar*" (found 6 times: Ezra 6:9; 7:22; Dan 5:1–2, 4, 23), and the Greek "oinos." Additional Hebrew expressions include "sobeʾ" (Isaiah 1:22; Hosea 4:18; Nahum 1:10) and "ḥemer" (Deuteronomy 32:14; Isaiah 27:2). The key words for new wine are Hebrew "tîrôš" (Isaiah 65:8; Hosea 9:2; Joel 2:24; Micah 6:15; Habakkuk 1:11; Zechariah 9:17) and Greek "oinos" (LXX), "oinos neos" (Matthew 9:17; Mark 2:22; Luke 5:37–39), and "gleukos" (Acts 2:13). A poetic synonym for "tîrôš" is "ʿāsîs" (Song of Solomon 8:2; Joel 1:5; 3[4]:18; Amos 9:13).

"New wine" denotes wine from the most recent harvest, while "old wine" refers to wine from the previous year's harvest. Old wine is favored for being sweeter and stronger (Sirach 9:10; Luke 5:39). At Qumran, new wine ("tîrôš") constituted their regular beverage (1QS 6:4–6; 1QSa 2:17–18, 20; 1QH 10:24). Although new wine was fermented, its ability to cause intoxication sets it apart (Isaiah 49:26; Hosea 4:11; Acts 2:13; cf. Judges 9:13). It fermented for a shorter duration compared to other wines (Joel 2:24), akin to a lower alcohol percentage (Isaiah 65:8; Micah 6:15). The LXX typically translates "tîrôš" as "oinos," indicating its fermented nature.

"Strong drink" (Hebrew "šēḵār," Greek "sikera") designates a fermented beverage made from barley, more resembling beer (Proverbs 20:1; Isaiah 24:9). The term is linked to "šāḵar," meaning "to be or become drunk" (Genesis 9:21; Isaiah 29:9; Jeremiah 25:27). Strong drink is undeniably intoxicating (Isaiah 28:7–8; 29:9; cf. 1 Samuel 1:15) and is consistently coupled with wine, often appearing in contexts warning against, forbidding, or denigrating their combined use (Leviticus 10:9; Numbers 6:3; Deuteronomy 29:6; Judges 13:4, 7, 14; 1 Samuel 1:15; Proverbs 20:1; 31:4, 6; Isaiah 5:11, 22; 24:9; 28:7; 29:9; 56:12; Micah 2:11; Luke 1:15; cf. Deuteronomy 14:26).

Synonyms for wine include the "blood of the grape" (Genesis 49:11; Deuteronomy 32:14; Sirach 39:26; 50:15), "fruit of the vine*" (Mark 14:25 par.; cf. Isaiah 32:12), or "the cup" (Mark 14:22–23 par.; 1 Corinthians 11:25). Wine is explicitly noted to be typically red (Proverbs 23:31). Indications of color include the red staining of winetreaders' clothing (Isaiah 63:2–3; cf. Revelation 14:20), the poetic synonym for wine as "the blood of grapes" (cf. Genesis 49:11–12), and the analogy of wine as blood at the Lord's Supper (cf. Mark 14:23–24 par; 1 Corinthians 11:25).

Wine could also be produced from pomegranates (Song of Solomon 8:2), raisins, apples, dates, honey, herbs, and figs. However, grape wine predominated. Classification of wine included factors such as color, age, and region of origin. Well-known varieties include the wine of Helbon (Ezekiel 27:18) and the wine of Lebanon (Hosea 14:7[8]).[2]

---

[2] D. F. Watson, "Wine," in Dictionary of Jesus and the Gospels, ed. Joel B. Green and Scot McKnight (Downers Grove, IL: InterVarsity Press, 1992), 870–871.

In Israel, the grape harvest unfolds in late August or September. In ancient times, the harvested fruit underwent a process of sun exposure for further ripening. Despite the later introduction of mechanical wine presses, during both the Old and New Testament periods, grapes were typically crushed by foot in vats—often circular basins carved from the bedrock. The initial crushing occurred in a primary vat, with the juice flowing through a channel to a secondary basin. This grape harvest was a festive occasion in Israel, marked by joyous celebrations and songs (Psalms 8, 81, 84 possibly being vintage songs; the term "Gittith" in their superscriptions might allude to the wine press, as in the LXX).

The fermentation process commenced almost immediately. The grape juice found storage in jars or goatskins, requiring new skins in the latter case to accommodate the expanding fermenting wine (Job 32:19; Mark 2:22). Once the wine was deemed ready, it underwent a preliminary straining with cloth to eliminate foreign matter and any remaining pulp (Matthew 23:24). Subsequently, it was poured into metal or pottery cups. Occasionally, spices were incorporated to enhance the taste (Song of Solomon 8:2). During New Testament times, the Romans infused their wine with scents like thyme, cinnamon, roses, and jasmine flowers. While wealthier Jews may have adopted this trend, the common person typically consumed their cup either in its natural state or with some honey. Although the Romans diluted their wine with water (2 Maccabees 15:39), such a practice was not the customary approach for the Jews (cf. Isaiah 1:22).

There is no biblical evidence supporting the notion that wine consisted solely of unfermented grape juice. Whenever the Bible mentions such juice (cf. Genesis 40:10–11), it is never referred to as wine. The term "new wine" (Hebrew: tîrôš; Micah 6:15; KJV, Isaiah 65:8; cf. Acts 2:13; Greek: gleúkos) also denoted fermented wine that could potentially intoxicate (Hosea 4:11; the LXX consistently translates tîrôš as Gk. oínos, meaning "wine"). New wine specifically pertained to the initial drippings from the vat, characterized by its purity and higher sugar content, leading to a more substantial fermented drink. This allowed for a grading system of wine (as seen in the wedding at Cana, where the steward discerns the quality; John 2:10).

In both the Old and New Testaments, wine holds a prominent place as a common aspect of life. It symbolizes well-being and God's blessings (Genesis 27:28), often serving as a gift (1 Samuel 25:18; 2 Samuel 16:1) and an article of trade (2 Chronicles 2:8–10 [MT 7–9]). Wine was reserved for festive occasions such as celebrations of circumcision, engagements, or marriages. It also featured prominently at annual festivals (Passover, Pentecost, Tabernacles) and during the Sabbath. Additionally, wine was recognized as a potent medicine (Luke 10:34; 1 Timothy 5:23; cf. Mishnah Šabb. xix.2, where wine is used in the healing of circumcision). When mixed with myrrh, it could serve as a narcotic, as exemplified in its offering to Jesus on the cross (Mark 15:23).

Wine played a role in Israelite rituals, functioning as a libation in sacrifice (Exodus 29:40; 1 Samuel 1:24). In the Hellenistic period, it might have been poured at the base of the altar, resembling blood (Sirach 50:15). This connection with sacrifice likely led to its inclusion in the Passover Seder (cf. Jubilees 49:6), and rabbinic requirements specified red wine for Passover (cf. Mishnah Pesaḥ vii.13, mentioning heated water for wine mixing). At Jesus's final Passover supper with his disciples, he explicitly connects wine to his blood, stating, "This (wine) is my blood of the covenant, which is poured out for many" (Mark 14:24 par.).

Abstinence from wine signified the piety of priests in service (Leviticus 10:9) and those under a Nazirite vow (Numbers 6:3). Rulers also received similar admonitions (Proverbs 31:4).

Although voluntary abstinence characterized figures like John the Baptist (Luke 1:15), it did not apply to Jesus. While Jesus was known for his willingness to drink wine, it might have subjected him to criticism (Luke 7:33–34; cf. John 2:1–11). Abstinence had historically been associated with religious zeal or piety, but Jesus refused to conform to traditional standards.

Despite being a divine gift and symbol of abundance, Scripture consistently warns against the abuse of wine (Isaiah 5:11; 28:7; Micah 2:11). Proverbs 23:29–35 serves as a virtual homily against drunkenness (cf. v. 20; 20:1; 21:17). The New Testament classifies such abuse as a serious sin (cf. Romans 13:13; 1 Corinthians 5:11; Galatians 5:21; 1 Peter 4:3), intolerable for those aspiring to inherit the kingdom of God (cf. 1 Corinthians 6:10). Consequently, church leaders must exercise moderation in their use of wine (1 Timothy 3:8; cf. Titus 2:3). Instead of becoming intoxicated with wine, Christians are urged to be "filled with the Spirit" (Ephesians 5:18). Paul advises that despite possessing freedom in Christ, it is appropriate to abstain from wine in the company of weaker Christians to prevent them from stumbling (Romans 14:21).[3]

---

[3] Allen C. Myers, The Eerdmans Bible Dictionary (Grand Rapids, MI: Eerdmans, 1987), 1058.

All Bible Verses Regarding Wine:

Gen 9:21 He drank of the wine and became drunk, and uncovered himself inside his tent.

Gen 9:24 When Noah awoke from his wine, he knew what his youngest son had done to him.

Gen 14:18 And Melchizedek king of Salem brought out bread and wine; now he was a priest of God Most High.

Gen 19:32 "Come, let us make our father drink wine, and let us lie with him that we may preserve our family through our father."

Gen 19:33 So they made their father drink wine that night, and the firstborn went in and lay with her father; and he did not know when she lay down or when she arose.

Gen 19:34 On the following day, the firstborn said to the younger, "Behold, I lay last night with my father; let us make him drink wine tonight also; then you go in and lie with him, that we may preserve our family through our father."

Gen 19:35 So they made their father drink wine that night also, and the younger arose and lay with him; and he did not know when she lay down or when she arose.

Gen 27:25 So he said, “Bring *it* to me, and I will eat of my son’s game, that I may bless you.” And he brought *it* to him, and he ate; he also brought him wine and he drank.

Gen 27:28 Now may God give you of the dew of heaven, And of the fatness of the earth, And an abundance of grain and new wine;

Gen 27:37 But Isaac replied to Esau, “Behold, I have made him your master, and all his relatives I have given to him as servants; and with grain and new wine I have sustained him. Now as for you then, what can I do, my son?”

Gen 49:11 “He ties *his* foal to the vine, And his donkey’s colt to the choice vine; He washes his garments in wine, And his robes in the blood of grapes.

Gen 49:12 “His eyes are dull from wine, And his teeth white from milk.

Exod 29:40 and there *shall be* one-tenth *of an ephah* of fine flour mixed with one-fourth of a hin of beaten oil, and one-fourth of a hin of wine for a drink offering with one lamb.

Lev 10:9 “Do not drink wine or strong drink, neither you nor your sons with you, when you come into the tent of meeting, so that you will not die—it is a perpetual statute throughout your generations—

Lev 23:13 'Its grain offering shall then be two-tenths *of an ephah* of fine flour mixed with oil, an offering by fire to the Lord *for* a soothing aroma, with its drink offering, a fourth of a hin of wine.

Num 6:3 he shall abstain from wine and strong drink; he shall drink no vinegar, whether made from wine or strong drink, nor shall he drink any grape juice nor eat fresh or dried grapes.

Num 6:20 'Then the priest shall wave them for a wave offering before the Lord. It is holy for the priest, together with the breast offered by waving and the thigh offered by lifting up; and afterward the Nazirite may drink wine.'

Num 15:5 and you shall prepare wine for the drink offering, one-fourth of a hin, with the burnt offering or for the sacrifice, for each lamb.

Num 15:7 and for the drink offering you shall offer one-third of a hin of wine as a soothing aroma to the Lord.

Num 15:10 and you shall offer as the drink offering one-half a hin of wine as an offering by fire, as a soothing aroma to the Lord.

Num 18:12 "All the best of the fresh oil and all the best of the fresh wine and of the grain, the first fruits of those which they give to the Lord, I give them to you.

Num 18:27 'Your offering shall be reckoned to you as the grain from the threshing floor or the full produce from the wine vat.

Num 18:30 "You shall say to them, 'When you have offered from it the best of it, then *the rest* shall be reckoned to the Levites as the product of the threshing floor, and as the product of the wine vat.

Num 28:14 'Their drink offerings shall be half a hin of wine for a bull and a third of a hin for the ram and a fourth of a hin for a lamb; this is the burnt offering of each month throughout the months of the year.

Deut 7:13 "He will love you and bless you and multiply you; He will also bless the fruit of your womb and the fruit of your ground, your grain and your new wine and your oil, the increase of your herd and the young of your flock, in the land which He swore to your forefathers to give you.

Deut 11:14 that He will give the rain for your land in its season, the early and late rain, that you may gather in your grain and your new wine and your oil.

Deut 12:17 "You are not allowed to eat within your gates the tithe of your grain
or new wine or oil, or the firstborn of your herd or flock, or any of your votive offerings which you

vow, or your freewill offerings, or the contribution of your hand.

Deut 14:23 “You shall eat in the presence of the Lord your God, at the place where He chooses to establish His name, the tithe of your grain, your new wine, your oil, and the firstborn of your herd and your flock, so that you may learn to fear the Lord your God always.

Deut 14:26 “You may spend the money for whatever your heart desires: for oxen, or sheep, or wine, or strong drink, or whatever your heart desires; and there you shall eat in the presence of the Lord your God and rejoice, you and your household.

Deut 15:14 “You shall furnish him liberally from your flock and from your threshing floor and from your wine vat; you shall give to him as the Lord your God has blessed you.

Deut 16:13 “You shall celebrate the Feast of Booths seven days after you have gathered in from your threshing floor and your wine vat;

Deut 18:4 “You shall give him the first fruits of your grain, your new wine, and your oil, and the first shearing of your sheep.

Deut 28:39 “You shall plant and cultivate vineyards, but you will neither drink of the wine nor gather *the grapes,* for the worm will devour them.

Deut 28:51 “Moreover, it shall eat the offspring of your herd and the produce of your ground until you are destroyed, who also leaves you no grain, new wine, or oil, nor the increase of your herd or the young of your flock until they have caused you to perish.

Deut 29:6 “You have not eaten bread, nor have you drunk wine or strong drink, in order that you might know that I am the Lord your God.

Deut 32:14 Curds of cows, and milk of the flock, With fat of lambs, And rams, the breed of Bashan, and goats, With the finest of the wheat— And of the blood of grapes you drank wine.

Deut 32:33 “Their wine is the venom of serpents, And the deadly poison of cobras.

Deut 32:38 ‘Who ate the fat of their sacrifices, *And* drank the wine of their drink offering? Let them rise up and help you, Let them be your hiding place!

Deut 33:28 “So Israel dwells in security, The fountain of Jacob secluded, In a land of grain and new wine; His heavens also drop down dew.

Judg 6:11 Then the angel of the Lord came and sat under the oak that was in Ophrah, which belonged to Joash the Abiezrite as his son Gideon was beating out wheat in the wine press in order to save it from the Midianites.

Judg 7:25 They captured the two leaders of Midian, Oreb and Zeeb, and they killed Oreb at the rock of Oreb, and they killed Zeeb at the wine press of Zeeb, while they pursued Midian; and they brought the heads of Oreb and Zeeb to Gideon from across the Jordan.

Judg 9:13 "But the vine said to them, 'Shall I leave my new wine, which cheers God and men, and go to wave over the trees?'

Judg 13:4 "Now therefore, be careful not to drink wine or strong drink, nor eat any unclean thing.

Judg 13:7 "But he said to me, 'Behold, you shall conceive and give birth to a son, and now you shall not drink wine or strong drink nor eat any unclean thing, for the boy shall be a Nazirite to God from the womb to the day of his death.' "

Judg 13:14 "She should not eat anything that comes from the vine nor drink wine or strong drink, nor eat any unclean thing; let her observe all that I commanded."

Judg 19:19 "Yet there is both straw and fodder for our donkeys, and also bread and wine for me, your maidservant, and the young man who is with your servants; there is no lack of anything."

1 Sam 1:14 Then Eli said to her, “How long will you make yourself drunk? Put away your wine from you.”

1 Sam 1:15 But Hannah replied, “No, my lord, I am a woman oppressed in spirit; I have drunk neither wine nor strong drink, but I have poured out my soul before the Lord.

1 Sam 1:24 Now when she had weaned him, she took him up with her, with a three-year-old bull and one ephah of flour and a jug of wine, and brought him to the house of the Lord in Shiloh, although the child was young.

1 Sam 10:3 “Then you will go on further from there, and you will come as far as the oak of Tabor, and there three men going up to God at Bethel will meet you, one carrying three young goats, another carrying three loaves of bread, and another carrying a jug of wine;

1 Sam 16:20 Jesse took a donkey *loaded with* bread and a jug of wine and a young goat, and sent *them* to Saul by David his son.

1 Sam 25:18 Then Abigail hurried and took two hundred *loaves* of bread and two jugs of wine and five sheep already prepared and five measures of roasted grain and a hundred clusters of raisins and two hundred cakes of figs, and loaded *them* on donkeys.

1 Sam 25:37 But in the morning, when the wine had gone out of Nabal, his wife told him these things, and his heart died within him so that he became *as* a stone.

2 Sam 13:28 Absalom commanded his servants, saying, “See now, when Amnon’s heart is merry with wine, and when I say to you, ‘Strike Amnon,’ then put him to death. Do not fear; have not I myself commanded you? Be courageous and be valiant.”

2 Sam 16:1 Now when David had passed a little beyond the summit, behold, Ziba the servant of Mephibosheth met him with a couple of saddled donkeys, and on them were two hundred loaves of bread, a hundred clusters of raisins, a hundred summer fruits, and a jug of wine.

2 Sam 16:2 The king said to Ziba, “Why do you have these?” And Ziba said, “The donkeys are for the king’s household to ride, and the bread and summer fruit for the young men to eat, and the wine, for whoever is faint in the wilderness to drink.”

2 Kings 6:27 He said, “If the Lord does not help you, from where shall I help you? From the threshing floor, or from the wine press?”

2 Kings 18:32 until I come and take you away to a land like your own land, a land of grain and new wine, a land of bread and vineyards, a land

of olive trees and honey, that you may live and not die." But do not listen to Hezekiah when he misleads you, saying, "The Lord will deliver us."

1 Chron 9:29 Some of them also were appointed over the furniture and over all the utensils of the sanctuary and over the fine flour and the wine and the oil and the frankincense and the spices.

1 Chron 12:40 Moreover those who were near to them, *even* as far as Issachar and Zebulun and Naphtali, brought food on donkeys, camels, mules and on oxen, great quantities of flour cakes, fig cakes and bunches of raisins, wine, oil, oxen and sheep. There was joy indeed in Israel.

1 Chron 27:27Shimei the Ramathite had charge of the vineyards; and Zabdi the Shiphmite had charge of the produce of the vineyards *stored* in the wine cellars.

2 Chron 2:10"Now behold, I will give to your servants, the woodsmen who cut the timber, 20,000 kors of crushed wheat and 20,000 kors of barley, and 20,000 baths of wine and 20,000 baths of oil."

2 Chron 2:15"Now then, let my lord send to his servants wheat and barley, oil and wine, of which he has spoken.

2 Chron 11:11He also strengthened the fortresses and put officers in them and stores of food, oil and wine.

2 Chron 31:5As soon as the order spread, the sons of Israel provided in abundance the first fruits of grain, new wine, oil, honey and of all the produce of the field; and they brought in abundantly the tithe of all.

2 Chron 32:28storehouses also for the produce of grain, wine and oil, pens for all kinds of cattle and sheepfolds for the flocks.

Ezra 6:9"Whatever is needed, both young bulls, rams, and lambs for a burnt offering to the God of heaven, and wheat, salt, wine and anointing oil, as the priests in Jerusalem request, *it* is to be given to them daily without fail,

Ezra 7:22*even* up to 100 talents of silver, 100 kors of wheat, 100 baths of wine, 100 baths of oil, and salt as needed.

Neh 2:1And it came about in the month Nisan, in the twentieth year of King Artaxerxes, that wine *was* before him, and I took up the wine and gave it to the king. Now I had not been sad in his presence.

Neh 5:11"Please, give back to them this very day their fields, their vineyards, their olive groves and their houses, also the hundredth *part* of the money and of the grain, the new wine and the oil that you are exacting from them."

Neh 5:15But the former governors who were before me laid burdens on the people and took from them bread and wine besides forty shekels of silver; even their servants domineered the people. But I did not do so because of the fear of God.

Neh 5:18Now that which was prepared for each day was one ox *and* six choice sheep, also birds were prepared for me; and once in ten days all sorts of wine *were furnished* in abundance. Yet for all this I did not demand the governor's food *allowance,* because the servitude was heavy on this people.

Neh 10:37 We will also bring the first of our dough, our contributions, the fruit of every tree, the new wine and the oil to the priests at the chambers of the house of our God, and the tithe of our ground to the Levites, for the Levites are they who receive the tithes in all the rural towns.

Neh 10:39 For the sons of Israel and the sons of Levi shall bring the contribution of the grain, the new wine and the oil to the chambers; there are the utensils of the sanctuary, the priests who are ministering, the gatekeepers and the singers. Thus we will not neglect the house of our God.

Neh 13:5 had prepared a large room for him, where formerly they put the grain offerings, the frankincense, the utensils and the tithes of grain, wine and oil prescribed for the Levites, the singers and the gatekeepers, and the contributions for the priests.

Neh 13:12 All Judah then brought the tithe of the grain, wine and oil into the storehouses.

Neh 13:15 In those days I saw in Judah some who were treading wine presses on the sabbath, and bringing in sacks of grain and loading *them* on donkeys, as well as wine, grapes, figs and all kinds of loads, and they brought *them* into Jerusalem on the sabbath day. So I admonished *them* on the day they sold food.

Esther 1:7Drinks were served in golden vessels of various kinds, and the royal wine was plentiful according to the king's bounty.

Esther 1:10 On the seventh day, when the heart of the king was merry with wine, he commanded Mehuman, Biztha, Harbona, Bigtha, Abagtha, Zethar and Carkas, the seven eunuchs who served in the presence of King Ahasuerus,

Esther 5:6 As they drank their wine at the banquet, the king said to Esther, "What is your petition, for it shall be granted to you. And what is your request? Even to half of the kingdom it shall be done."

Esther 7:1 Now the king and Haman came to drink *wine* with Esther the queen.

Esther 7:2 And the king said to Esther on the second day also as they drank their wine at the banquet, "What is your petition, Queen Esther? It shall be granted you. And what is your request? Even to half of the kingdom it shall be done."

Esther 7:7 The king arose in his anger from drinking wine *and went* into the palace garden; but Haman stayed to beg for his life from Queen Esther, for he saw that harm had been determined against him by the king.

Esther 7:8 Now when the king returned from the palace garden into the place where they were drinking wine, Haman was falling on the couch where Esther was. Then the king said, "Will he even assault the queen with me in the house?" As the word went out of the king's mouth, they covered Haman's face.

Job 1:13 Now on the day when his sons and his daughters were eating and drinking wine in their oldest brother's house,

Job 1:18 While he was still speaking, another also came and said, "Your sons and your daughters were eating and drinking wine in their oldest brother's house,

Job 24:11 "Within the walls they produce oil; They tread wine presses but thirst.

Job 32:19 "Behold, my belly is like unvented wine, Like new wineskins it is about to burst.

Ps 4:7 You have put gladness in my heart, More than when their grain and new wine abound.

Ps 60:3 You have made Your people experience hardship; You have given us wine to drink that makes us stagger.

Ps 75:8 For a cup is in the hand of the Lord, and the wine foams; It is well mixed, and He pours out of this; Surely all the wicked of the earth must drain *and* drink down its dregs.

Ps 78:65 Then the Lord awoke as *if from* sleep, Like a warrior overcome by wine.

Ps 104:15 And wine which makes man's heart glad, So that he may make *his* face glisten with oil, And food which sustains man's heart.

Prov 3:10 So your barns will be filled with plenty And your vats will overflow with new wine.

Prov 4:17 For they eat the bread of wickedness And drink the wine of violence.

Prov 9:2 She has prepared her food, she has mixed her wine; She has also set her table;

Prov 9:5 “Come, eat of my food And drink of the wine I have mixed.

Prov 21:17 He who loves pleasure *will become* a poor man; He who loves wine and oil will not become rich.

Prov 23:20 Do not be with heavy drinkers of wine, *Or* with gluttonous eaters of meat;

Prov 23:30 Those who linger long over wine, Those who go to taste mixed wine.

Prov 23:31 Do not look on the wine when it is red, When it sparkles in the cup, When it goes down smoothly;

Prov 31:4 It is not for kings, O Lemuel, It is not for kings to drink wine, Or for rulers to desire strong drink,

Prov 31:6 Give strong drink to him who is perishing, And wine to him whose life is bitter.

Eccles 2:3 I explored with my mind *how* to stimulate my body with wine while my mind was guiding *me* wisely, and how to take hold of folly, until I could see what good there is for the sons of men to do under heaven the few years of their lives.

Eccles 9:7 Go *then,* eat your bread in happiness and drink your wine with a cheerful heart; for God has already approved your works.

Eccles 10:19 *Men* prepare a meal for enjoyment, and wine makes life merry, and money is the answer to everything.

Song 1:2 "May he kiss me with the kisses of his mouth! For your love is better than wine.

Song 1:4 "Draw me after you *and* let us run *together!* The king has brought me into his chambers." "We will rejoice in you and be glad; We will extol your love more than wine. Rightly do they love you."

Song 4:10 "How beautiful is your love, my sister, *my* bride! How much better is your love than wine, And the fragrance of your oils Than all *kinds* of spices!

Song 5:1 "I have come into my garden, my sister, *my* bride; I have gathered my myrrh along with my balsam. I have eaten my honeycomb and my honey; I have drunk my wine and my milk. Eat, friends; Drink and imbibe deeply, O lovers."

Song 7:2 "Your navel is *like* a round goblet Which never lacks mixed wine; Your belly is like a heap of wheat Fenced about with lilies.

Song 7:9 And your mouth like the best wine!" "It goes *down* smoothly for my beloved, Flowing gently *through* the lips of those who fall asleep.

Song 8:2“ I would lead you *and* bring you Into the house of my mother, who used to instruct me; I would give you spiced wine to drink from the juice of my pomegranates.

Isa 5:2 He dug it all around, removed its stones, And planted it with the choicest vine. And He built a tower in the middle of it And also hewed out a wine vat in it; Then He expected *it* to produce *good* grapes, But it produced *only* worthless ones.

Isa 5:10“ For ten acres of vineyard will yield *only* one bath *of wine,* And a homer of seed will yield *but* an ephah of grain.”

Isa 5:11 Woe to those who rise early in the morning that they may pursue strong drink, Who stay up late in the evening that wine may inflame them!

Isa 5:12 Their banquets are *accompanied* by lyre and harp, by tambourine and flute, and by wine; But they do not pay attention to the deeds of the Lord, Nor do they consider the work of His hands.

Isa 5:22 Woe to those who are heroes in drinking wine And valiant men in mixing strong drink,

Isa 16:10 Gladness and joy are taken away from the fruitful field; In the vineyards also there will be no cries of joy or jubilant shouting, No treader treads out wine in the presses, *For* I have made the shouting to cease.

Isa 22:13 Instead, there is gaiety and gladness, Killing of cattle and slaughtering of sheep, Eating of meat and drinking of wine: "Let us eat and drink, for tomorrow we may die."

Isa 24:7 The new wine mourns, The vine decays, All the merry-hearted sigh.

Isa 24:9 They do not
drink wine with song; Strong drink is bitter to those who drink it.

Isa 24:11 There is an outcry in the streets concerning the wine; All joy turns to gloom. The gaiety of the earth is banished.

Isa 25:6 The Lord of hosts will prepare a lavish banquet for all peoples on this mountain; A banquet of aged wine, choice pieces with marrow, *And* refined, aged wine.

Isa 27:2 In that day, "A vineyard of wine, sing of it!

Isa 28:1 Woe to the proud crown of the drunkards of Ephraim, And to the fading flower of its glorious beauty, Which is at the head of the fertile valley Of those who are overcome with wine!

Isa 28:7 And these also reel with wine and stagger from strong drink: The priest and the prophet reel with strong drink, They are confused by wine, they stagger from strong drink; They reel while having visions, They totter *when rendering* judgment.

Isa 29:9 Be delayed and wait, Blind yourselves and be blind; They become drunk, but not with wine, They stagger, but not with strong drink.

Isa 36:17 until I come and take you away to a land like your own land, a land of grain and new wine, a land of bread and vineyards.

Isa 49:26 “I will feed your oppressors with their own flesh, And they will become drunk with their own blood as with sweet wine; And all flesh will know that I, the Lord, am your Savior And your Redeemer, the Mighty One of Jacob.”

Isa 51:21 Therefore, please hear this, you afflicted, Who are drunk, but not with wine:

Isa 55:1 “Ho! Every one who thirsts, come to the waters; And you who have no money come, buy and eat. Come, buy wine and milk Without money and without cost.

Isa 56:12 “Come,” *they say,* “let us get wine, and let us drink heavily of strong drink; And tomorrow will be like today, only more so.”

Isa 62:8 The Lord has sworn by His right hand and by His strong arm, “I will never again give your grain *as* food for your enemies; Nor will foreigners drink your new wine for which you have labored."

Isa 63:2 Why is Your apparel red, And Your garments like the one who treads in the wine press?

Isa 63:3 "I have trodden the wine trough alone, And from the peoples there was no man with Me. I also trod them in My anger And trampled them in My wrath; And their lifeblood is sprinkled on My garments, And I stained all My raiment.

Isa 65:8 Thus says the Lord, "As the new wine is found in the cluster, And one says, 'Do not destroy it, for there is benefit in it,' So I will act on behalf of My servants In order not to destroy all of them.

Isa 65:11 "But you who forsake the Lord, Who forget My holy mountain, Who set a table for Fortune, And who fill *cups* with mixed wine for Destiny,

Jer 13:12 "Therefore you are to speak this word to them, 'Thus says the Lord, the God of Israel, "Every jug is to be filled with wine." ' And when they say to you, 'Do we not very well know that every jug is to be filled with wine?'

Jer 23:9 As for the prophets: My heart is broken within me, All my bones tremble; I have become like a drunken man, Even like a man overcome with wine, Because of the Lord And because of His holy words.

Jer 25:15 For thus the Lord, the God of Israel, says to me, "Take this cup of the wine of wrath from My hand and cause all the nations to whom I send you to drink it.

Jer 31:12 "They will come and shout for joy on the height of Zion, And they will be radiant over the bounty of the Lord— Over the grain and the new wine and the oil, And over the young of the flock and the herd; And their life will be like a watered garden, And they will never languish again.

Jer 35:2 "Go to the house of the Rechabites and speak to them, and bring them into the house of the Lord, into one of the chambers, and give them wine to drink."

Jer 35:5 Then I set before the men of the house of the Rechabites pitchers full of wine and cups; and I said to them, "Drink wine!"

Jer 35:6 But they said, "We will not drink wine, for Jonadab the son of Rechab, our father, commanded us, saying, 'You shall not drink wine, you or your sons, forever.

Jer 35:8 "We have obeyed the voice of Jonadab the son of Rechab, our father, in all that he commanded us, not to drink wine all our days, we, our wives, our sons or our daughters,

Jer 35:14 "The words of Jonadab the son of Rechab, which he commanded his sons not to drink wine, are observed. So they do not drink *wine* to this day, for they have obeyed their father's command. But I have spoken to you again and again; yet you have not listened to Me.

Jer 40:10 "Now as for me, behold, I am going to stay at Mizpah to stand *for you* before the Chaldeans who come to us; but as for you, gather in wine and summer fruit and oil and put *them* in your *storage* vessels, and live in your cities that you have taken over."

Jer 40:12 Then all the Jews returned from all the places to which they had been driven away and came to the land of Judah, to Gedaliah at Mizpah, and gathered in wine and summer fruit in great abundance.

Jer 48:11 "Moab has been at ease since his youth; He has also been undisturbed, *like wine* on its dregs, And he has not been emptied from vessel to vessel, Nor has he gone into exile. Therefore he retains his flavor, And his aroma has not changed.

Jer 48:33 "So gladness and joy are taken away From the fruitful field, even from the land of

Moab. And I have made the wine to cease from the wine presses; No one will tread *them* with shouting, The shouting will not be shouts *of joy.*

Jer 51:7 Babylon has been a golden cup in the hand of the Lord, Intoxicating all the earth. The nations have drunk of her wine; Therefore the nations are going mad.

Lam 1:15 "The Lord has rejected all my strong men In my midst; He has called an appointed time against me To crush my young men; The Lord has trodden *as in* a wine press The virgin daughter of Judah.

Lam 2:12 They say to their mothers, "Where is grain and wine?" As they faint like a wounded man In the streets of the city, As their life is poured out On their mothers' bosom.

Ezek 27:18 "Damascus was your customer because of the abundance of your goods, because of the abundance of all *kinds* of wealth, because of the wine of Helbon and white wool.

Ezek 44:21 "Nor shall any of the priests drink wine when they enter the inner court.

Dan 1:5 The king appointed for them a daily ration from the king's choice food and from the wine which he drank, and *appointed* that they should be educated three years, at the end of which they were to enter the king's personal service.

Dan 1:8 But Daniel made up his mind that he would not defile himself with the king's choice food or with the wine which he drank; so he sought *permission* from the commander of the officials that he might not defile himself.

Dan 1:16 So the overseer continued to withhold their choice food and the wine they were to drink, and kept giving them vegetables.

Dan 5:1 Belshazzar the king held a great feast for a thousand of his nobles, and he was drinking wine in the presence of the thousand.

Dan 5:2 When Belshazzar tasted the wine, he gave orders to bring the gold and silver vessels which Nebuchadnezzar his father had taken out of the temple which *was* in Jerusalem, so that the king and his nobles, his wives and his concubines might drink from them.

Dan 5:4 They drank the wine and praised the gods of gold and silver, of bronze, iron, wood and stone.

Dan 5:23 but you have exalted yourself against the Lord of heaven; and they have brought the vessels of His house before you, and you and your nobles, your wives and your concubines have been drinking wine from them; and you have praised the gods of silver and gold, of bronze, iron, wood and stone, which do not see, hear or understand. But the God in whose hand are your life-breath and all your ways, you have not glorified.

Dan 10:3 I did not eat any tasty food, nor did meat or wine enter my mouth, nor did I use any ointment at all until the entire three weeks were completed.

Hos 2:8 “For she does not know that it was I who gave her the grain, the new wine and the oil, And lavished on her silver and gold, *Which* they used for Baal.

Hos 2:9 “Therefore, I will take back My grain at harvest time And My new wine in its season. I will also take away My wool and My flax *Given* to cover her nakedness.

Hos 2:22 And the earth will respond to the grain, to the new wine and to the oil, And they will respond to Jezreel.

Hos 4:11 Harlotry, wine and new wine take away the understanding.

Hos 7:5 On the day of our king, the princes became sick with the heat of wine; He stretched out his hand with scoffers,

Hos 7:14 And they do not cry to Me from their heart When they wail on their beds; For the sake of grain and new wine they assemble themselves, They turn away from Me.

Hos 9:2 Threshing floor and wine press will not feed them, And the new wine will fail them.

Hos 9:4 They will not pour out drink offerings of wine to the Lord, Their sacrifices will not please Him. *Their bread will be* like mourners' bread; All who eat of it will be defiled, For their bread will be for themselves *alone;* It will not enter the house of the Lord.

Hos 14:7 Those who live in his shadow Will again raise grain, And they will blossom like the vine. His renown *will be* like the wine of Lebanon.

Joel 1:5 Awake, drunkards, and weep; And wail, all you wine drinkers, On account of the sweet wine That is cut off from your mouth.

Joel 1:10The field is ruined, The land mourns; For the grain is ruined, The new wine dries up, Fresh oil fails.

Joel 2:19 The Lord will answer and say to His people, "Behold, I am going to send you grain, new wine and oil, And you will be satisfied *in full* with them; And I will never again make you a reproach among the nations.

Joel 2:24 The threshing floors will be full of grain, And the vats will overflow with the new wine and oil.

Joel 3:3 “They have also cast lots for My people, Traded a boy for a harlot And sold a girl for wine that they may drink.

Joel 3:13 Put in the sickle, for the harvest is ripe. Come, tread, for the wine press is full; The vats overflow, for their wickedness is great.

Joel 3:18 And in that day The mountains will drip with sweet wine, And the hills will flow with milk, And all the brooks of Judah will flow with water; And a spring will go out from the house of the Lord To water the valley of Shittim.

Amos 2:8 “On garments taken as pledges they stretch out beside every altar, And in the house of their God they drink the wine of those who have been fined.

Amos 2:12 “But you made the Nazirites drink wine, And you commanded the prophets saying, ‘You shall not prophesy!’

Amos 5:11 Therefore because you impose heavy rent on the poor And exact a tribute of grain from them, *Though* you have built houses of well-hewn stone, Yet you will not live in them; You have planted pleasant vineyards, yet you will not drink their wine.

Amos 6:6 Who drink wine from sacrificial bowls While they anoint themselves with the finest of oils, Yet they have not grieved over the ruin of Joseph.

Amos 9:13 “Behold, days are coming,” declares the Lord, “When the plowman will overtake the reaper And the treader of grapes him who sows seed; When the mountains will drip sweet wine And all the hills will be dissolved.

Amos 9:14 “Also I will restore the captivity of My people Israel, And they will rebuild the ruined cities and live *in them;* They will also plant vineyards and drink their wine, And make gardens and eat their fruit.

Micah 2:11 “If a man walking after wind and falsehood Had told lies *and said,* ‘I will speak out to you concerning wine and liquor,’ He would be spokesman to this people.

Micah 6:15 “You will sow but you will not reap. You will tread the olive but will not anoint yourself with oil; And the grapes, but you will not drink wine.

Hab 2:5 “Furthermore, wine betrays the haughty man, So that he does not stay at home. He enlarges his appetite like Sheol, And he is like death, never satisfied. He also gathers to himself all nations And collects to himself all peoples.

Zeph 1:13 “Moreover, their wealth will become plunder And their houses desolate; Yes, they will build houses but not inhabit *them,* And plant vineyards but not drink their wine.”

Haggai 1:11 “I called for a drought on the land, on the mountains, on the grain, on the new wine, on the oil, on what the ground produces, on men, on cattle, and on all the labor of your hands.”

Haggai 2:12 ‘If a man carries holy meat in the fold of his garment, and touches bread with this fold, or cooked food, wine, oil, or any *other* food, will it become holy?’ ” And the priests answered, “No.”

Haggai 2:16 from that time *when* one came to a *grain* heap of twenty *measures,* there would be only ten; and *when* one came to the wine vat to draw fifty measures, there would be *only* twenty.

Zech 9:15 The Lord of hosts will defend them. And they will devour and trample on the sling stones; And they will drink *and* be boisterous as with wine; And they will be filled like a *sacrificial* basin, *Drenched* like the corners of the altar.

Zech 9:17 For what comeliness and beauty *will be* theirs! Grain will make the young men flourish, and new wine the virgins.

Zech 10:7 “Ephraim will be like a mighty man, And their heart will be glad as if *from* wine; Indeed, their children will see *it* and be glad, Their heart will rejoice in the Lord.

Zech 14:10 All the land will be changed into a plain from Geba to Rimmon south of Jerusalem; but Jerusalem will rise and remain on its site from Benjamin's Gate as far as the place of the First Gate to the Corner Gate, and from the Tower of Hananel to the king's wine presses.

Matt 9:17 "Nor do *people* put new wine into old wineskins; otherwise the wineskins burst, and the wine pours out and the wineskins are ruined; but they put new wine into fresh wineskins, and both are preserved."

Matt 21:33 "Listen to another parable. There was a landowner
who planted a vineyard and put a wall around it and dug a wine press in it, and built a tower, and rented it out to vine-growers and went on a journey.

Matt 27:34 they gave Him wine to drink mixed with gall; and after tasting *it,* He was unwilling to drink.

Matt 27:48 Immediately one of them ran, and taking a sponge, he filled it with sour wine and put it on a reed, and gave Him a drink.

Mark 2:22 "No one puts new wine into old wineskins; otherwise the wine will burst the skins, and the wine is lost and the skins *as well;* but *one puts* new wine into fresh wineskins."

Mark 12:1 And He began to speak to them in parables: "A
man planted a vineyard and put a wall around it, and dug a vat under the wine press and built a to wer, and rented it out to vine-growers and went on a journey.

Mark 15:23 They tried to give Him wine mixed with myrrh; but He did not take it.

Mark 15:36 Someone ran and filled a sponge with sour wine, put it on a reed, and gave Him a drink, saying, "Let us see whether Elijah will come to take Him down."

Luke 1:15 "For he will be great in the sight of the Lord; and he will drink no wine or liquor, and he will be filled with the Holy Spirit while yet in his mother's womb.

Luke 5:37 "And no one puts new wine into old wineskins; otherwise the new wine will burst the skins and it will be spilled out, and the skins will be ruined.

Luke 5:3 8 "But new wine must be put into fresh wineskins.

Luke 5:39 "And no one, after drinking
old *wine* wishes for new; for he says, 'The old is good *enough*.' "

Luke 7:33 “For John the Baptist has come eating no bread and drinking no wine, and you say, ‘He has a demon!’

Luke 10:34 and came to him and bandaged up his wounds, pouring oil and wine on *them;* and he put him on his own beast, and brought him to an inn and took care of him.

Luke 23:36 The soldiers also mocked Him, coming up to Him, offering Him sour wine,

John 2:3 When the wine ran out, the mother of Jesus said to Him, “They have no wine.”

John 2:9 When the headwaiter tasted the water which had become wine, and did not know where it came from (but the servants who had drawn the water knew), the headwaiter called the bridegroom,

John 2:10 and said to him, “Every man serves the good wine first, and when *the people* have drunk freely, *then he serves* the poorer *wine; but* you have kept the good wine until now.”

John 4:46 Therefore He came again to Cana of Galilee where He had made the water wine. And there was a royal official whose son was sick at Capernaum.

John 19:29 A jar full of sour wine was standing there; so they put a sponge full of the sour wine upon *a branch of* hyssop and brought it up to His mouth.

John 19:30 Therefore when Jesus had received the sour wine, He said, "It is finished!" And He bowed His head and gave up His spirit.

Acts 2:13 But others were mocking and saying, "They are full of sweet wine."

Rom 14:21 It is good not to eat meat or to drink wine, or *to do anything* by which your brother stumbles.

Eph 5:18 And do not get drunk with wine, for that is dissipation, but be filled with the Spirit,

1 Tim 3:3 not addicted to wine or pugnacious, but gentle, peaceable, free from the love of money.

1 Tim 3:8 Deacons likewise *must be* men of dignity, not double-tongued, or addicted to much wine or fond of sordid gain,

1 Tim 5:23 No longer drink water *exclusively,* but use a little wine for the sake of your stomach and your frequent ailments.

Titus 1:7 For the overseer must be above reproach as God's steward, not self-willed, not quick-tempered, not addicted to wine, not pugnacious, not fond of sordid gain,

Titus 2:3 Older women likewise are to be reverent in their behavior, not malicious gossips nor enslaved to much wine, teaching what is good,

Rev 6:6 And I heard *something* like a voice in the center of the four living creatures saying, “A quart of wheat for a denarius, and three quarts of barley for a denarius; and do not damage the oil and the wine.”

Rev 14:8 And another angel, a second one, followed, saying, “Fallen, fallen is Babylon the great, she who has made all the nations drink of the wine of the passion of her immorality.”

Rev 14:10 he also will drink of the wine of the wrath of God, which is mixed in full strength in the cup of His anger; and he will be tormented with fire and brimstone in the presence of the holy angels and in the presence of the Lamb.

Rev 14:19 So the angel swung his sickle to the earth and gathered *the clusters from* the vine of the earth, and threw them into the great wine press of the wrath of God.

Rev 14:20 And the wine press was trodden outside the city, and blood came out from the wine press, up to the horses’ bridles, for a distance of two hundred miles.

Rev 16:19 The great city was split into three parts, and the cities of the nations fell. Babylon the great was remembered before God, to give her the cup of the wine of His fierce wrath.

Rev 17:2 with whom the kings of the earth committed *acts of* immorality, and those who dwell on the earth were made drunk with the wine of her immorality."

Rev 18:3 "For all the nations have drunk of the wine of the passion of her immorality, and the kings of the earth have committed *acts of* immorality with her, and the merchants of the earth have become rich by the wealth of her sensuality."

Rev 18:13 and cinnamon and spice and incense and perfume and frankincense and wine and olive oil and fine flour and wheat and cattle and sheep, and *cargoes* of horses and chariots and slaves and human lives.

Rev 19:15 From His mouth comes a sharp sword, so that with it He may strike down the nations, and He will rule them with a rod of iron; and He treads the wine press of the fierce wrath of God, the Almighty.

Printed in Great Britain
by Amazon

42073129R00050